The TOOLIEZ

Written by Alonzo Herran

Illustrated by Alonzo Herran, Ronald Austin and Marvin Charles

Edited by Azizah Y. Mohammed-Tsabet and Kamilah Yasin

Dear Parents:

The Tooliez Books are specifically designed to provide new and creative ways to help build your child's mind, body and spirit. Our goal is to promote character building for children so that they may have a better relationship with family and friends and uphold good spiritual values. Tooliez World LLC seeks to reinforce the tools of discipline, honesty, respect, confidence, wisdom, humility, and creativity. The Tooliez workbook provides easy color-in illustrations, fun fill-ins, quick quizzes, wonderful work projects, and creative sound suggestions.

We encourage you and your child to explore these exercises together. We believe that the skills taught in this book will help your child to discover more about him/herself, and you will learn more about your child. The skills will also help children to live a positive and productive life.

The Tooliez Tool-Rific OATH

™

This book belongs to:

_____

I, _____ , agree to follow my parents' rules and try my best to complete the exercises in this book. I promise to show love, honesty and dedication in all that I do and to practice the values of The Tooliez so that I can become a member of The Tooliez Tool-Rific Club.

_____   _____

Member's Signature   Date

_____   _____

Parent's Signature   Date

The Introduction of Tools

Since the beginning of time, nothing has been created with a higher intelligence than the human being. Humans have battled the earth, wind, fire and water. In order to survive, people created tools to provide food, shelter and clothing. Tools often reflect the needs of people, their personalities, and the environment (world around us). They help us to achieve our goals.

Without tools,
humans are limited.
Without humans,
tools are limited.

The spirit of tools has always been with us. Some tools help our minds. Other tools help our bodies. Many tools help us work in the world around us. We even have tools to help us grow in the spiritual world (or life). Now it's time to see how humans and tools become one so that parents and children can build relationships to prepare for the future.

The Tooliez Beginning

Seven young, troubled students decided to change the course of their lives. They made a promise to graduate from college so that they could make a positive impact in the world.

After graduating from college and working in their professions for several years, the friends reunited to vacation on an island. They went hiking in the mountains and during their explorations, they discovered a special box buried in the mud. As the friends attempted to open the box with different tools, something caused the box to explode. The explosion triggered a bright, radioactive light that covered them with Atomic Bionic Connectors and transformed the seven young professionals into the tools they were holding! They had become part human and part tool with super abilities. They were no longer ordinary professionals. They became...The Tooliez!

Let's discover these new characters and get to know their personalities and superpowers.

THE TOOLBOX

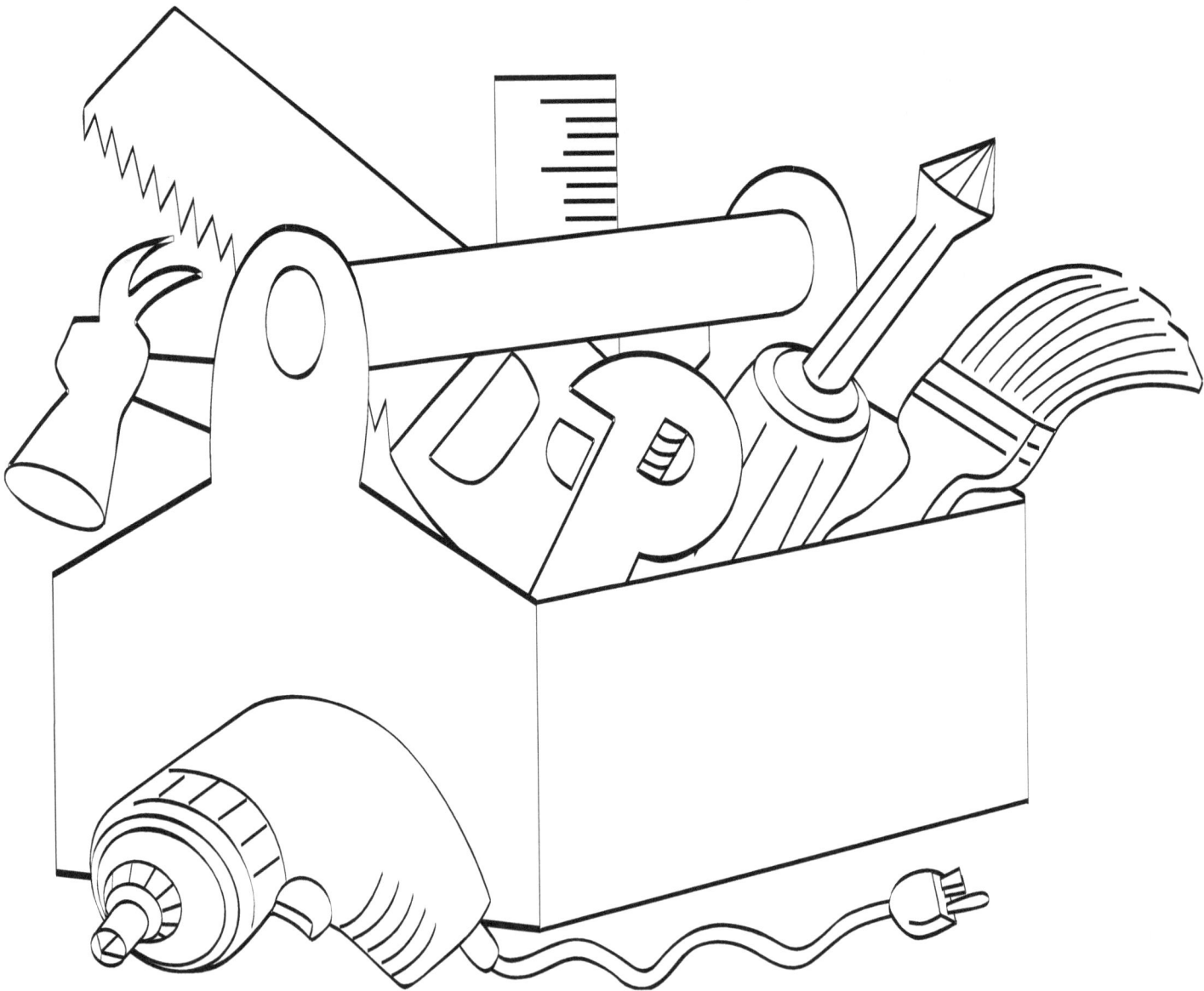

A toolbox is a case or container used to hold or carry tools.

THE DRILL

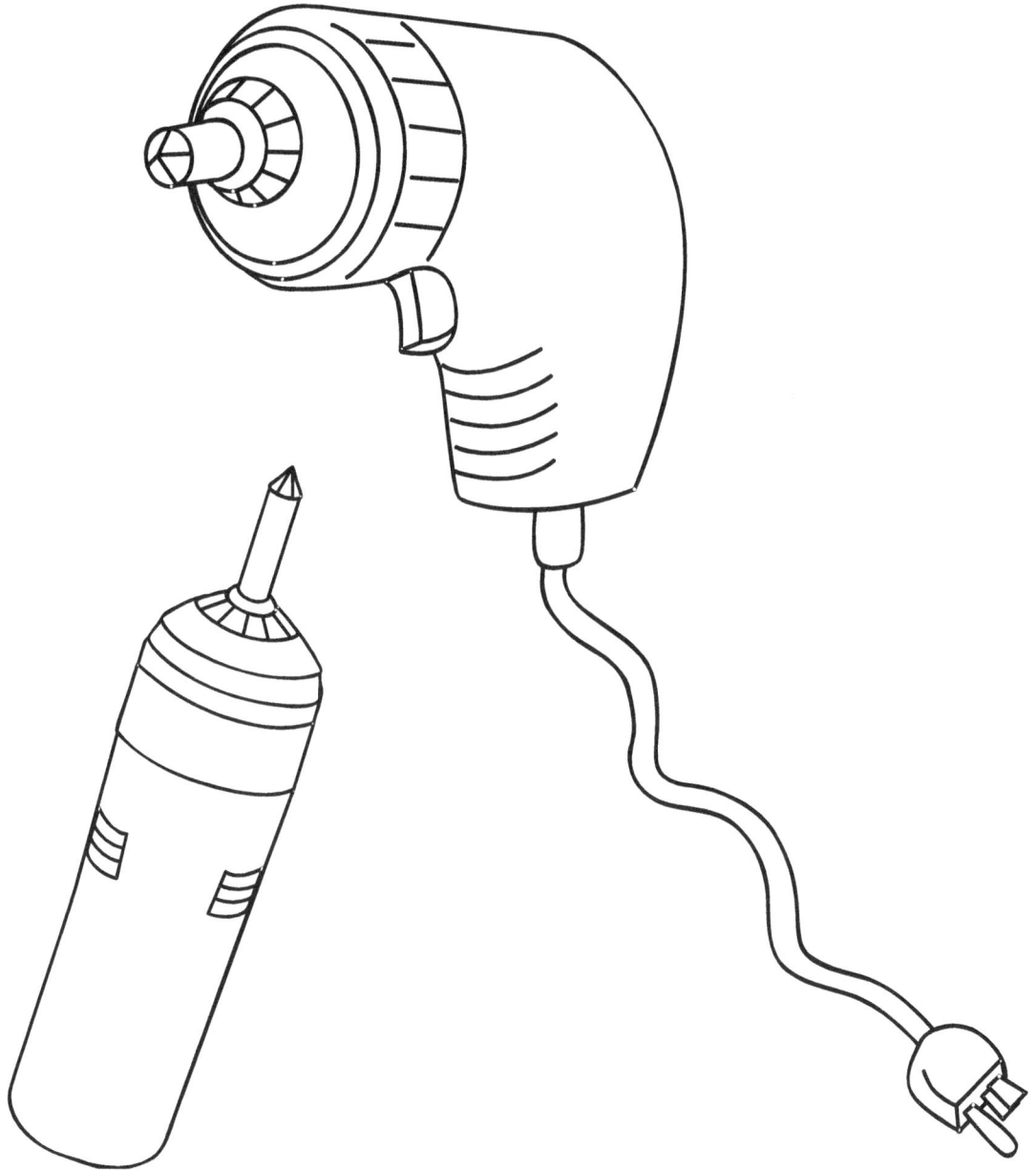

A drill is a power tool that is used to make holes in materials such as wood, metal and stone.

Sgt. Drill Bit

PERSONALITY: Sgt. Drill Bit is the tool of Discipline. He is highly motivated, organized and tough. He loves to maintain order.

ADVICE: To be a good leader, you must be a good follower. Listen to your parents and teachers and set good examples for your siblings and other relatives, friends and classmates.

Sgt. Drill Bit

SUPERPOWER: Sgt. Drill Bit has the power to fly into action as he faces challenges and achieves his goals.

ADVICE: Find the power within yourself to be the best you can be. Never quit.

Building Discipline with Sgt. Drill Bit

DAILY ROUTINE DRILLS

Choose from these words to complete the sentences below. Answers are at the bottom of the page.

Permission	Dignity	Steal	Organized	Respect
Honor	Good	Lies	Clean	Thankful

1. I will _____ my faith, family and country every day of my life.

2. I will _____ my family, friends and people who are different from me.

3. I will not tell _____ to myself or to others for any reason.

4. I will not _____ or take any object unless it is given to me.

5. I will not go anywhere or do anything without my parents' _____ .

6. I will be _____ for any food that's on my plate.

7. I promise to brush my teeth and keep my body _____ daily.

8. I will wear my clothes with _____ .

9. I promise to be _____ in school, listen to my teacher, study hard, and do my homework.

10. I will do my chores and keep my room _____ and neat.

Your greatest fears can be your greatest challenges.
Name your fears and what you can do to overcome them.

1. _____

2. _____

Answer Key: (1) Honor (2) Respect (3) Lies (4) Steal (5) Permission (6) Thankful (7) Clean (8) Dignity (9) Good (10) Organized

THE HAMMER

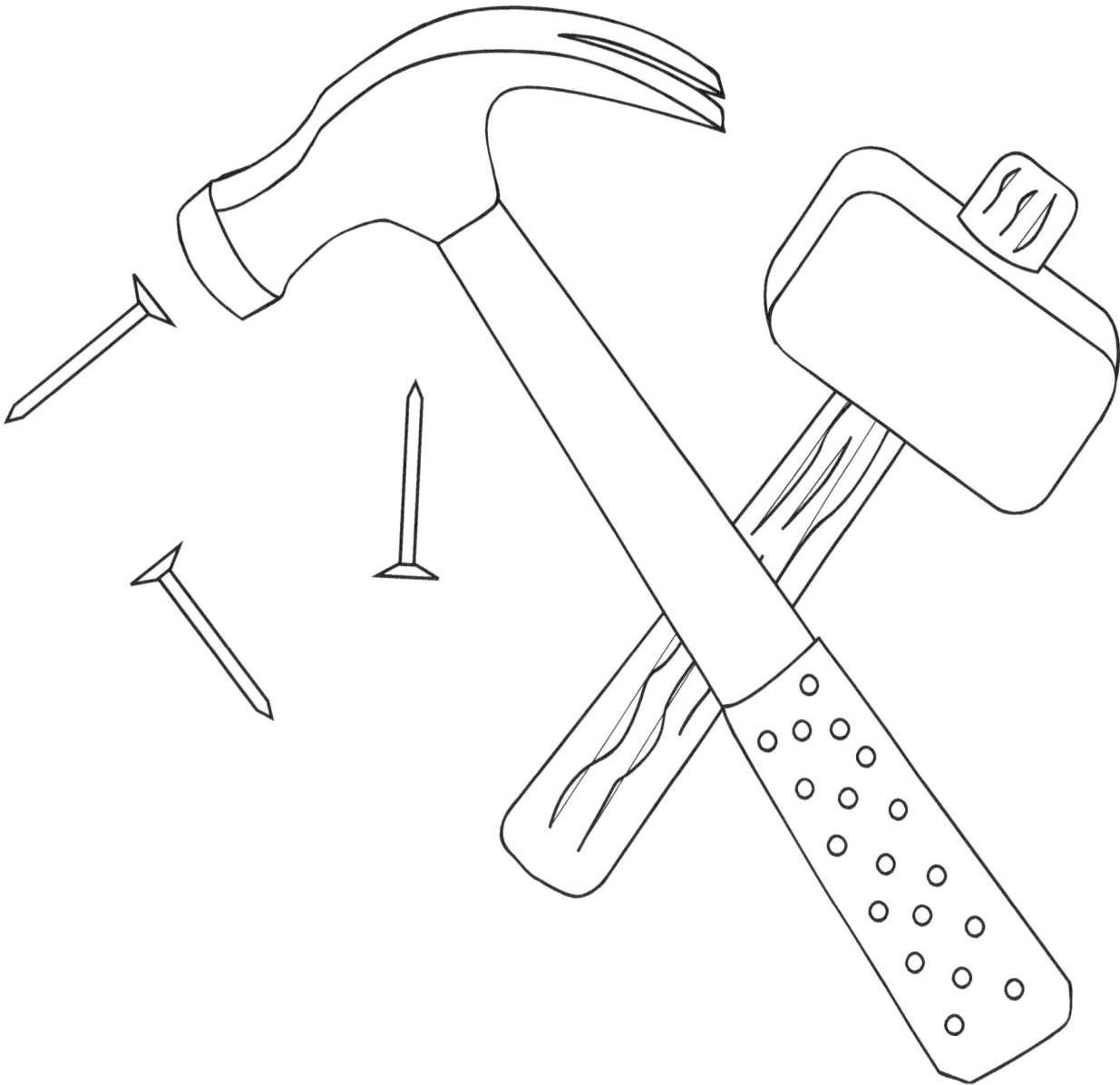

A hammer is a heavy tool used for hitting nails into wood or walls.

Hammie

PERSONALITY: Hammie is the tool of Honesty. She is focused and believes in telling the truth at all times.

ADVICE: Always be truthful. Never steal, lie or cheat to get your way. The truth will set you free.

Hammie

SUPERPOWER: Hammie can use her hammer to create a shock wave to protect herself and her friends from any negative attacks.

ADVICE: Find the power within yourself to always defend the truth, even if you stand alone.

Building Honesty with Hammie
THE VALUE OF TELLING THE TRUTH

Always express your true thoughts and feelings.

1 = a	10 = j	19 = s
2 = b	11 = k	20 = t
3 = c	12 = l	21 = u
4 = d	13 = m	22 = v
5 = e	14 = n	23 = w
6 = f	15 = o	24 = x
7 = g	16 = p	25 = y
8 = h	17 = q	26 = z
9 = i	18 = r	

Match the letters to the numbers and write the secret message!

```
___   ___ ___ ___ ___
 1     8   1   12  6

___ ___ ___ ___ ___     ___ ___     ___
20  18  21  20  8        9   19       1

___ ___ ___ ___ ___     ___ ___ ___
23   8  15  12  5        12  9   5
```

THE SAW

A saw is a tool with a jagged blade and a handle used to cut wood.

Cutter

PERSONALITY: Cutter is the tool of Respect. Sometimes he is mean and stubborn, and has to be reminded to be respectful.

ADVICE: Treat others the way you want to be treated. Do not threaten, hit or hurt anyone.

Cutter

SUPERPOWER: Cutter has the power to cut through anything and the ability to run with lightning speed.

ADVICE: Find the power within yourself to cut the negative behaviors from your life. Run away from influences that will get you into trouble.

Building Respect with Cutter

YOU HAVE TO EARN RESPECT

We can sometimes show *respect* or *disrespect* to others by the way we move our bodies. Let's identify some good conduct and other behaviors we should try to avoid as we interact with others.

Body Language	
Placing hands on hips	Hugging
Nodding	Smiling
Rolling one's eyes	Interrupting someone who is speaking
Turning one's back while another speaks	Waving
Shaking hands	Looking into a speaker's eyes
Pointing finger in someone's face	Clenching fists

Write down the words and phrases from above in the correct column below.

Respectful Body Language	Disrespectful Body Language

Respect – you must give it to get it

THE SCREWDRIVER

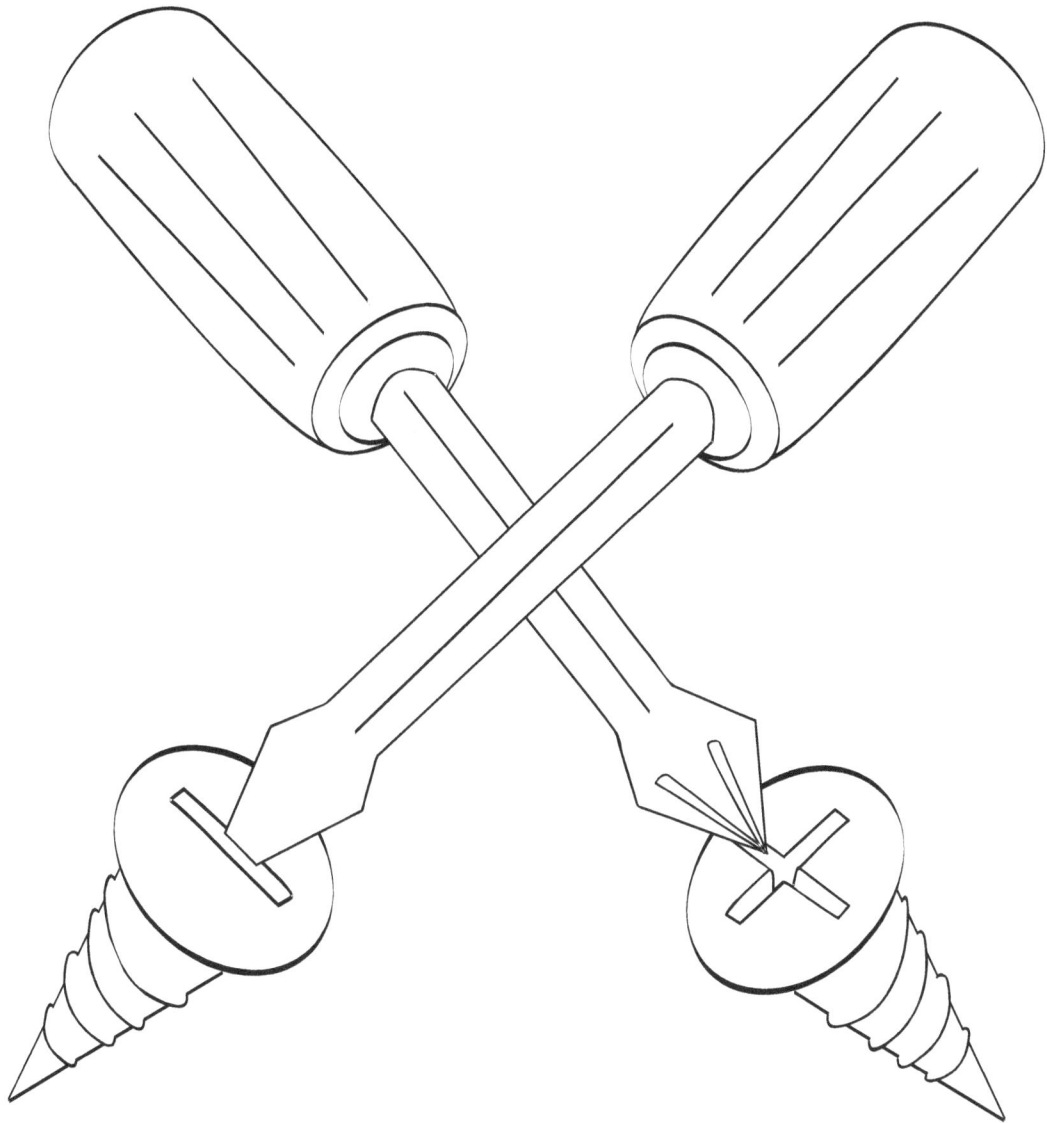

A screwdriver is a tool for tightening or loosening screws. It has a thin, wedge-shaped end which fits into the groove of a screw head.

Screwee

PERSONALITY: Screwee is the tool of Confidence. He is funny, silly and energetic. He has a dual personality: he is either calm and focused, or wild and misbehaved.

ADVICE: Be brave and face your fears. It is all right to act silly and have fun at the right time and place.

Screwee

SUPERPOWER: Screwee has the power to create a tornado while spinning extremely fast.

ADVICE: Find the power within yourself to think before you speak, and think before you act. Be sure of yourself and show your talents to others.

Building Confidence with Screwee

THINK BEFORE YOU ACT

Find your way through the maze.

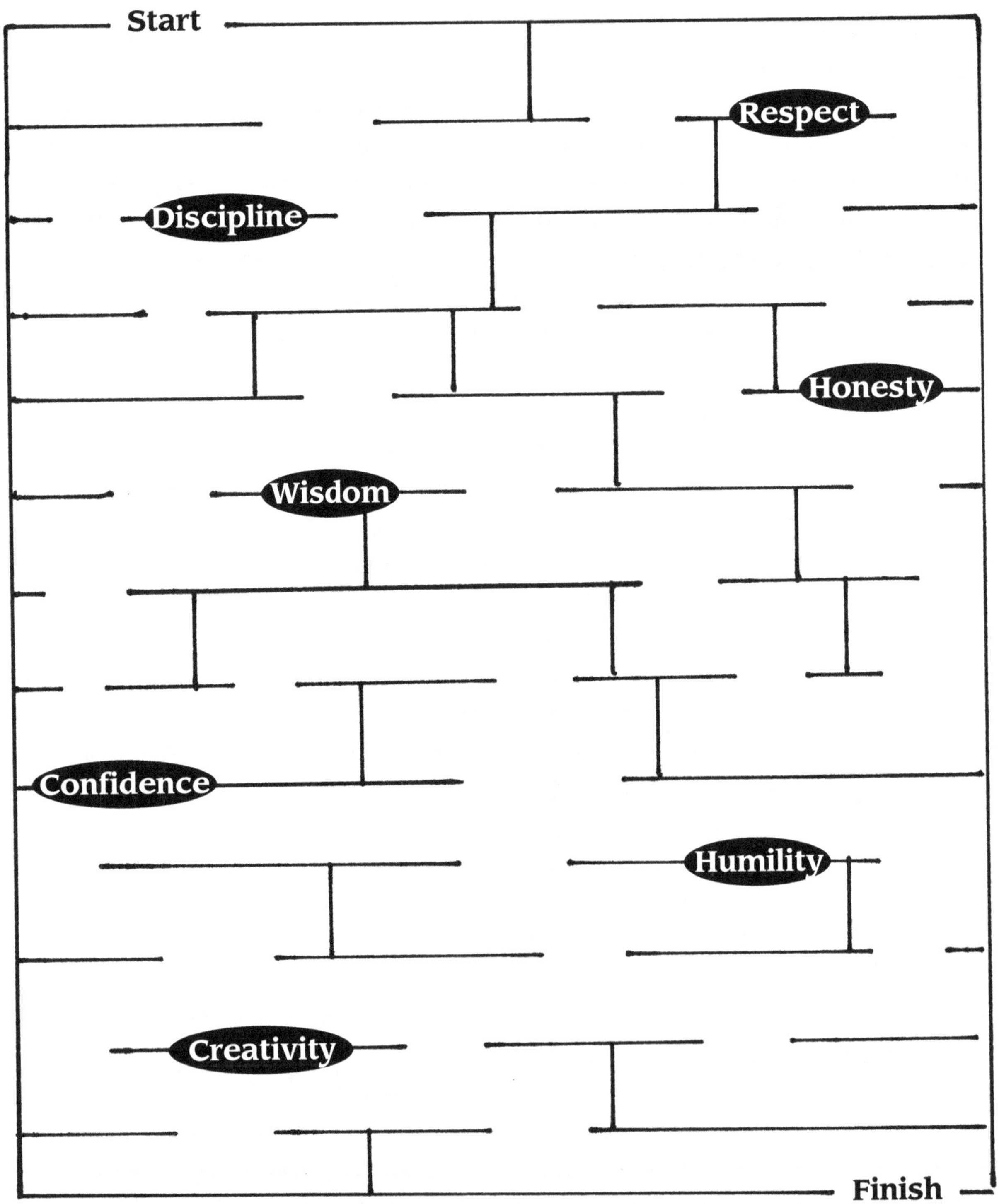

Start

Respect

Discipline

Honesty

Wisdom

Confidence

Humility

Creativity

Finish

THE RULER

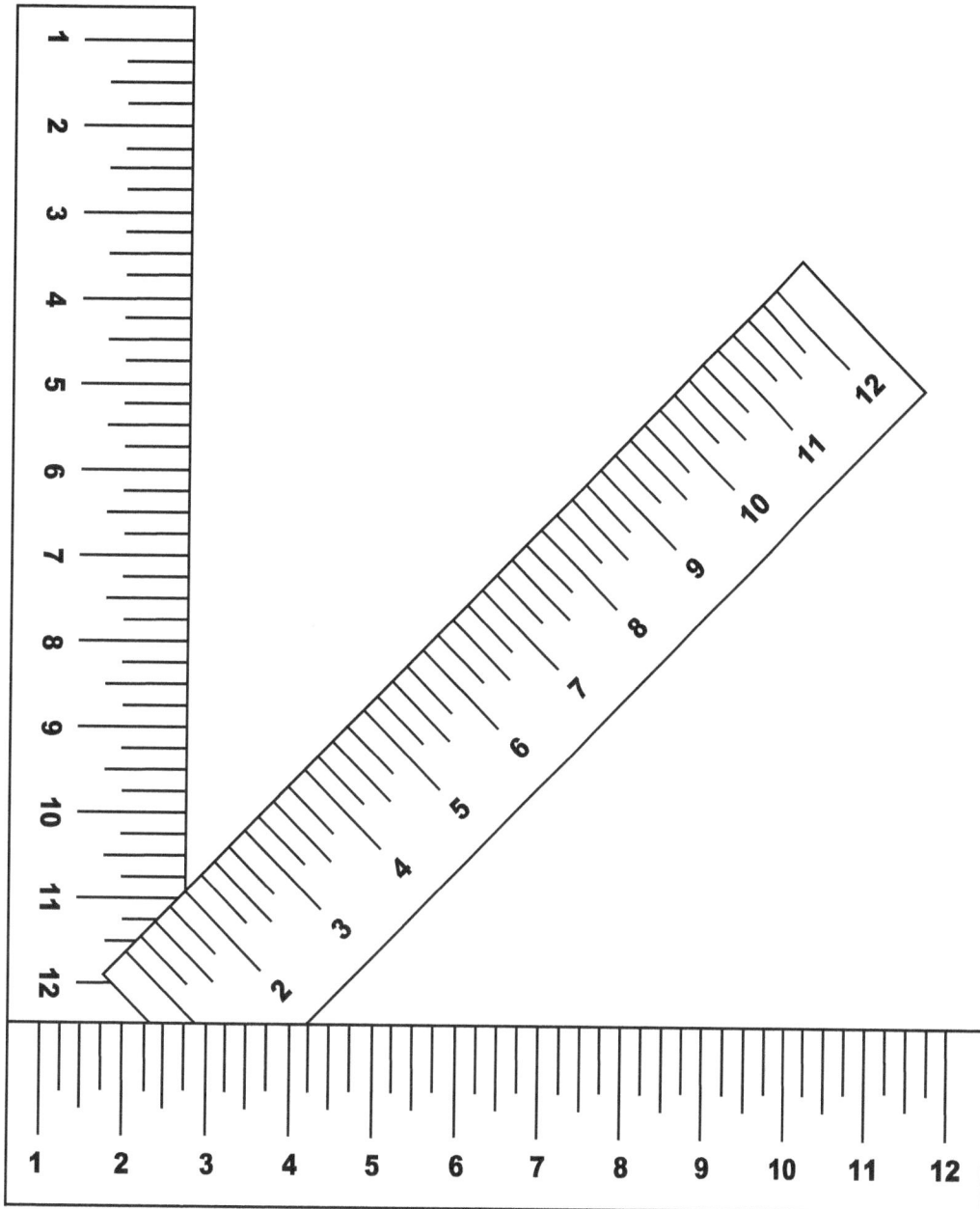

A ruler is a strip of wood, metal or plastic with a straight edge that is marked off in inches and/or centimeters. It is used to measure lengths, widths and heights.

Ruly

PERSONALITY: Ruly is the tool of Wisdom. He is smart, accurate, intelligent, and sophisticated.

ADVICE: Excellent grades are earned by working, not by playing around. Read and study every day.

Ruly

SUPERPOWER: Ruly has the power to stretch his mind and body to give accurate solutions to any questions or problems.

ADVICE: Find the power within yourself to study hard and seek knowledge above and beyond your grade level. Remember, wisdom is power: the more you know, the further you will go.

How many words can you make using the letters in:

strengthen vocabulary

1. _____   11. _____

2. _____   12. _____

3. _____   13. _____

4. _____   14. _____

5. _____   15. _____

6. _____   16. _____

7. _____   17. _____

8. _____   18. _____

9. _____   19. _____

10. _____   20. _____

Fun Learning Games –

1. Reading – Read books on different topics and act out stories for your family and friends.

2. Vocabulary – Ask your family and teachers for new words to look up in a dictionary. Take part in a weekly spelling bee at home.

3. Writing – Express your thoughts in a journal or diary and try to use new vocabulary words.

4. Math – Pretend that you are a calculator and practice solving math problems provided by your teachers and family.

THE WRENCH

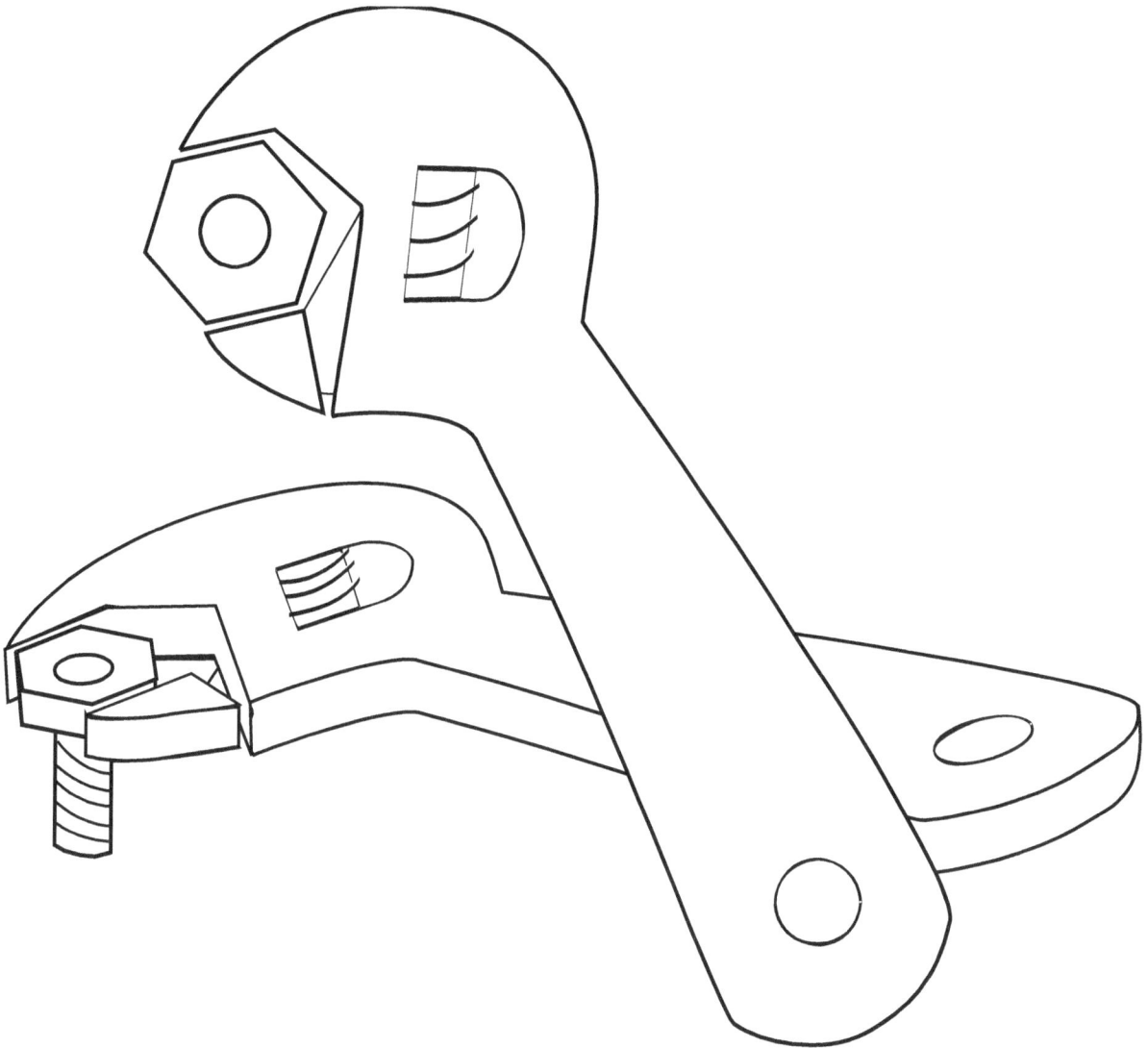

A wrench is a tool with adjustable jaws for gripping and turning objects such as nuts or bolts.

Gripper

PERSONALITY: Gripper is the tool of Humility. He is strong, shy and humble. He is a peacemaker and enjoys connecting objects together.

ADVICE: A part of life is knowing that everyone makes mistakes. When you make a mistake, you can learn from that experience. Be a part of the solution, not a part of the problem.

Gripper

SUPERPOWER: Gripper has the power to double or shrink his size and strength by using his special coat to help others in danger.

ADVICE: Use your strength to improve yourself, others and your surroundings. Help people in need and protect the environment.

Building Humility with Gripper
FIND YOUR STRENGTH WITHIN

Unscramble the letters below to spell ten words that describe humility, one of the seven characteristics of The Tooliez.

1. I D <u>N</u> K _____

2. H L E F <u>P</u> U L _____

3. <u>A</u> C N G I <u>R</u> _____

4. H <u>S</u> N G A R I _____

5. V I G N G <u>I</u> _____

6. P R <u>S</u> U T V E P O <u>I</u> _____

7. <u>O</u> I G L V N _____

8. T H G F <u>O</u> H U T U L _____

9. E K E <u>M</u> _____

10. <u>C</u> N E R E N D O C _____

Now, unscramble the bold, underlined letters above to create another word to describe an important quality that a humble person has toward others:

____ ____ ____ ____ ____ ____ ____ ____ ____

Answer Key: (1) Kind (2) Helpful (3) Caring (4) Sharing (5) Giving (6) Supportive, (7) Loving (8) Thoughtful (9) Meek (10) Concerned. Compassion

30

THE PAINTBRUSH

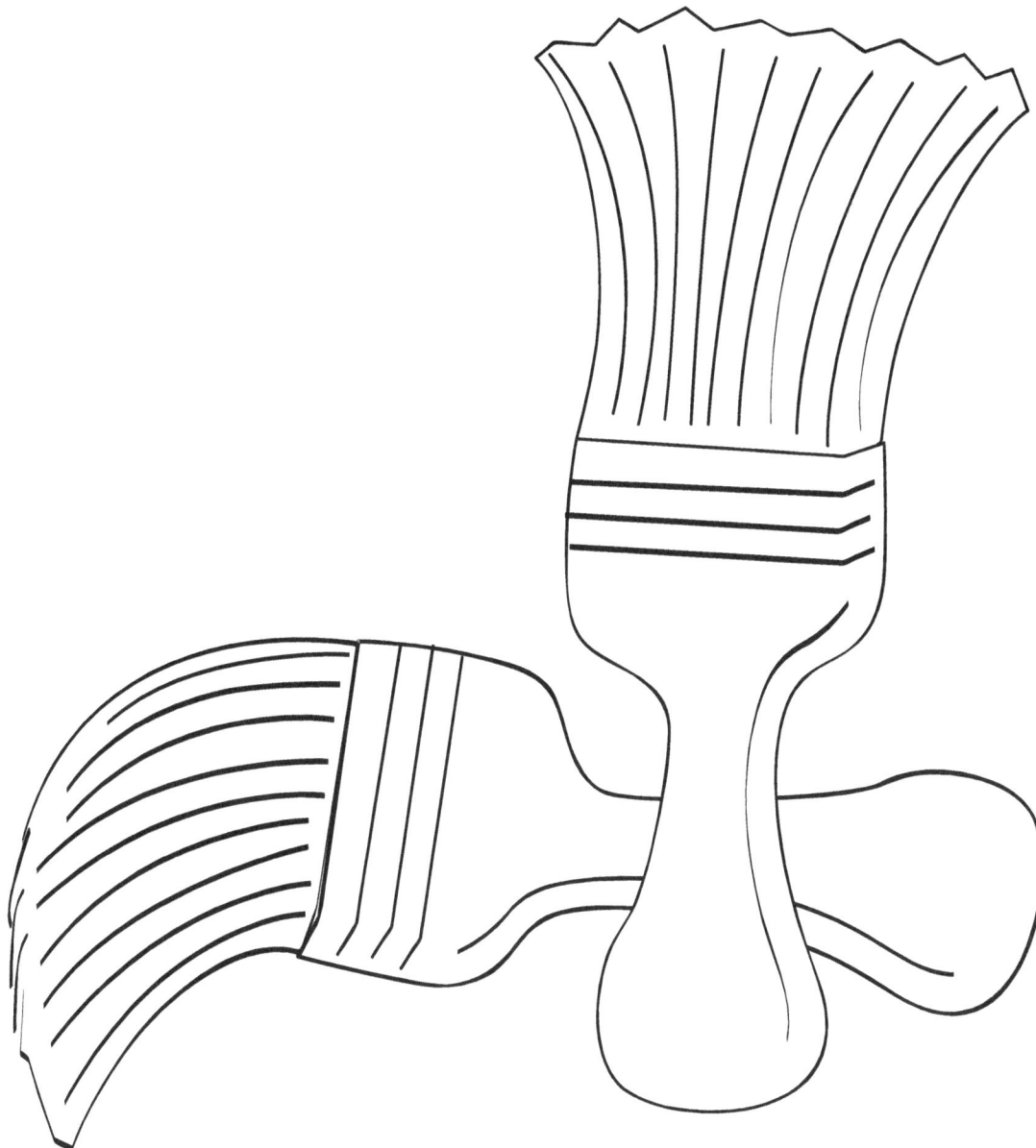

A paintbrush is a tool with many stiff hairs that are joined to a handle. It is used to apply paint to walls and other surfaces.

Beutie

PERSONALITY: Beutie is the tool of Creativity. She is glamorous, conceited and artistic.

ADVICE: Everyone has ideas, visions and dreams. Do not let anyone or anything prevent you from pursuing your goals.

Beutie

SUPERPOWER: Beutie has the power to adapt to her surroundings and bring life to the pictures she paints.

ADVICE: Find the power within yourself to express your gifts and talents and make your dreams come true.

Building Creativity with Beutie
FIND WAYS TO ENJOY YOUR DAYS

Write or draw whatever you are thinking at this very moment.

You may never know if you can write a story or draw unless you try.

Create a family or community service project.

1. Ask your parents to help you to bake a cake or cookies for someone you love.

2. Ask your parents what chores you can do to help them around the house.

3. Ask your parents how you can help a friend or someone in need.

Make the best of every day by using your gifts and talents to better yourself and others.

THE SEVEN BASIC TOOLS

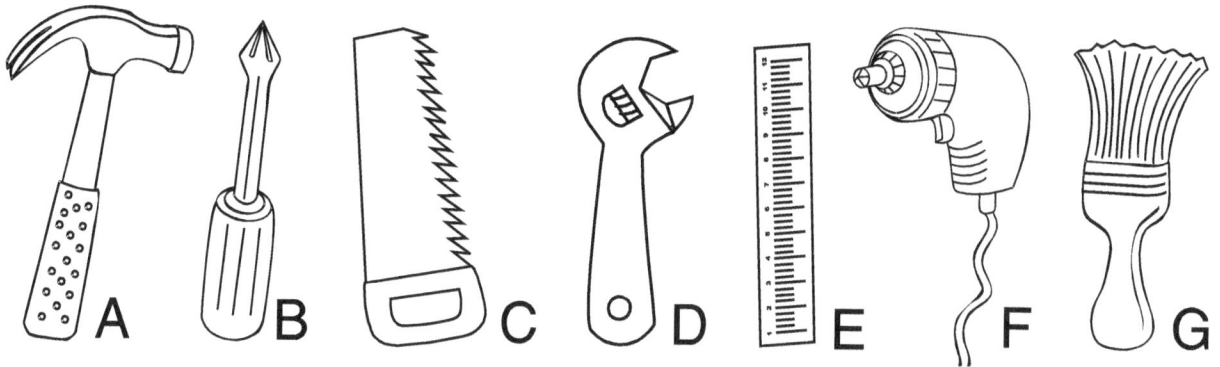

A   B   C   D   E   F   G

Write the letter of the tool you would use to ...

1. Make a hole _____

2. Connect bolts and nuts _____

3. Cut wood and sheetrock _____

4. Tighten or loosen screws _____

5. Measure space and distance _____

6. Drive nails into a wall _____

7. Paint a wall or picture _____

CHARACTER WORD SEARCH

Find and circle the 7 Principles of The Tooliez:
DISCIPLINE, HONESTY, RESPECT, CONFIDENCE, WISDOM,
HUMILITY, and CREATIVITY.

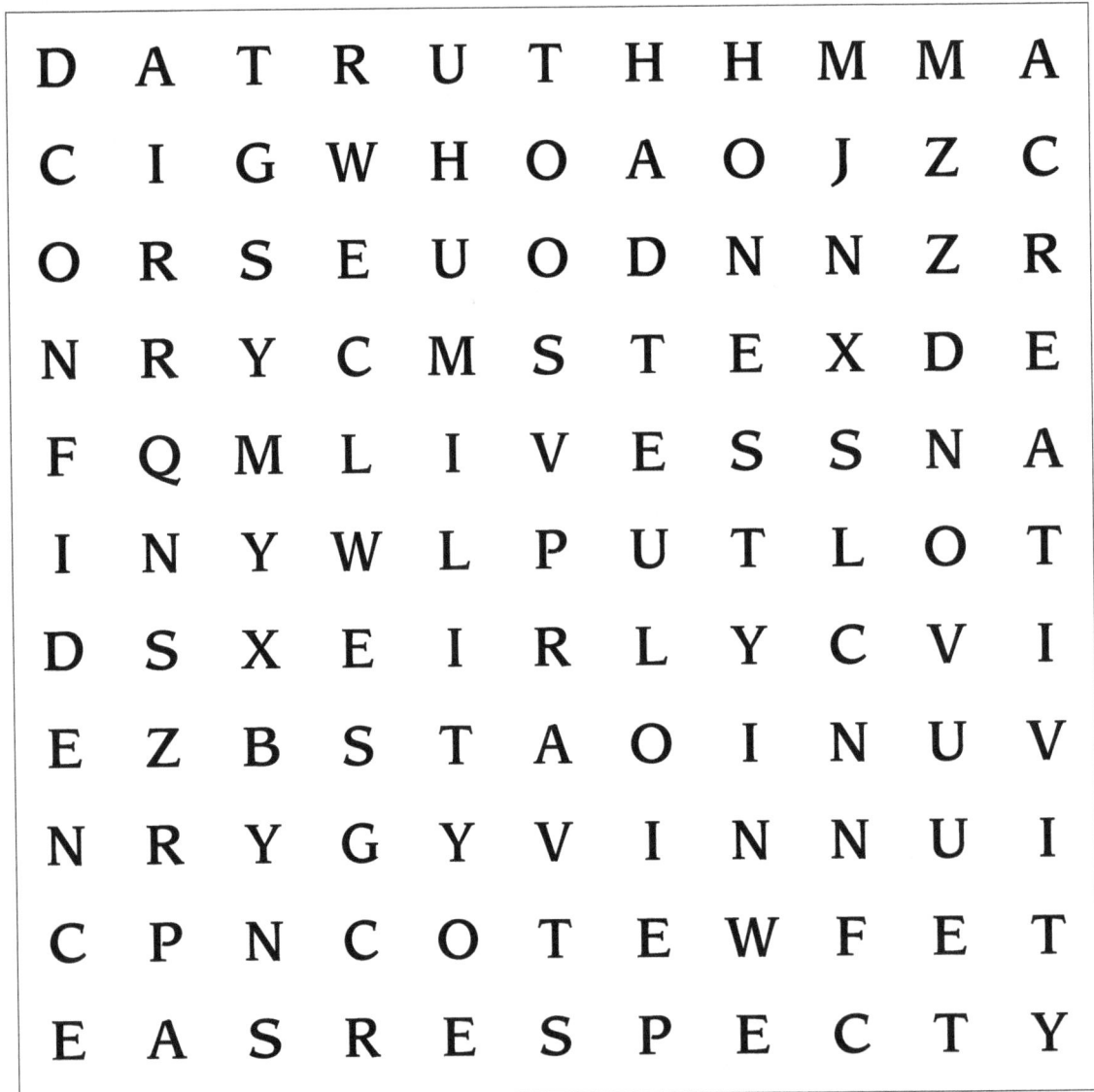

```
D  A  T  R  U  T  H  H  M  M  A
C  I  G  W  H  O  A  O  J  Z  C
O  R  S  E  U  O  D  N  N  Z  R
N  R  Y  C  M  S  T  E  X  D  E
F  Q  M  L  I  V  E  S  S  N  A
I  N  Y  W  L  P  U  T  L  O  T
D  S  X  E  I  R  L  Y  C  V  I
E  Z  B  S  T  A  O  I  N  U  V
N  R  Y  G  Y  V  I  N  N  U  I
C  P  N  C  O  T  E  W  F  E  T
E  A  S  R  E  S  P  E  C  T  Y
```

Parents can only give good advice or put them on the right paths,
but the final forming of a person's character lies in their own hands.
— *Anne Frank*

CROSSWORD PUZZLE

Use the Clues Below to Complete the Puzzle

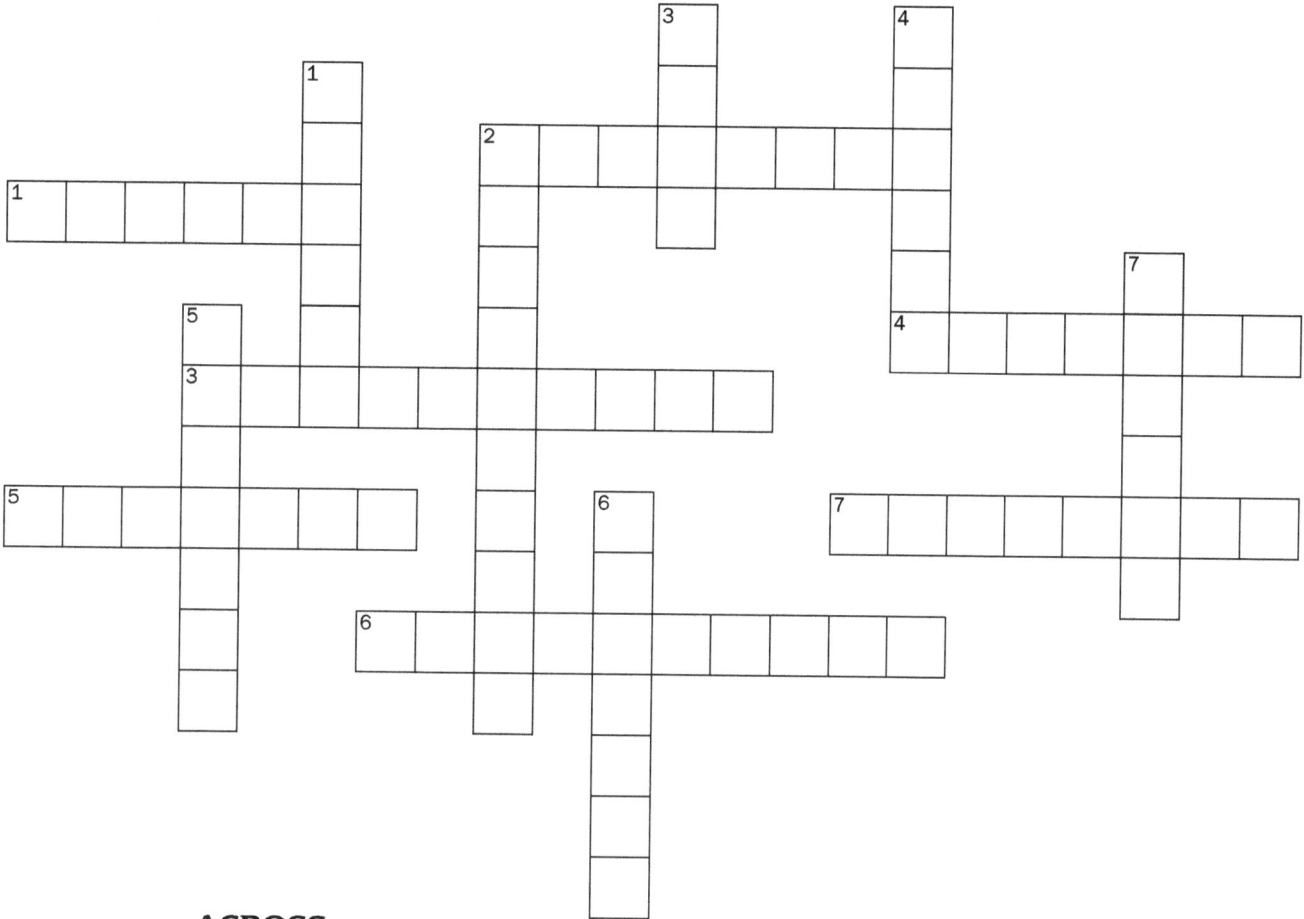

ACROSS

1. A person with great knowledge and judgment has _____ .

2. He is the leader of The Tooliez Team.

3. A word that means great imagination.

4. When you listen to and obey your parents and teachers, you show them _____ .

5. _____ is when someone tells the truth.

6. When someone is sure of himself, he has _____ .

7. Understanding of other people's needs.

DOWN

1. She can make a shock wave.

2. Character trait that means focused and organized.

3. He can stretch his body.

4. He can cut, slice and dice any object.

5. He can create a tornado.

6. He is super big and strong.

7. She loves to create colorful pieces of work.

THIS IS WHO I AM

Please complete this informational form and record important facts about yourself. This form will help you to learn more about yourself and help your parents to learn more about you.

Name: _____

Address: _____

Phone Numbers: _____

My Birthday: _____

My Place of Birth: _____

My Family Members: _____

My Family Origin: _____

My Race: _____

My Faith: _____

My School: _____

My Favorite Subject: _____

My Favorite Food: _____

My Favorite Color: _____

My Favorite Friend: _____

My Favorite Book: _____

My Favorite Game: _____

My Favorite Movies: _____

My Favorite Trip: _____

Once you complete this task, you may move onto the next challenge. We recommend that you update this information every 6 months to see how you change and grow over the years.

MY TRUE FEELINGS

This is a 3-part challenge. Please be honest in completing this task so that you can grow based on the answers you give.

A. Write the top 10 character traits that you...

Like About Yourself	**Would Like To Improve In Yourself**
1. _____	1. _____
2. _____	2. _____
3. _____	3. _____
4. _____	4. _____
5. _____	5. _____
6. _____	6. _____
7. _____	7. _____
8. _____	8. _____
9. _____	9. _____
10. _____	10. _____

B. Ask your parents, family and friends the same questions about yourself.

1. Do any of their answers match your answers?_____

2. Are there any character traits that you need to improve?_____

C. Which character trait will you try to improve first? How will you improve this trait?_____

_____

CIRCLE OF FRIENDS

We all have a group of friends whom we talk and play with. Most circles of friends consist of people from our own race, ethnic group or culture. This Tooliez task would like to help you to think about adding friends from other races, cultures or ethnic groups to your circle. Let's try it!

What is your ethnic background?_____

How many friends do you have and play with?_____

What are your friends' ethnic backgrounds?_____

_____

What other states or countries are your friends and their families from?

_____

What does it mean to you to have friends from other races, cultures or ethnic groups?

_____

_____

Let's make your circle of friends bigger and better. Here are 4 ways to make friends and build relationships with others who are different from you.

1. **Meet** and **Greet** other kids who are different from you

2. **Exchange** and **Participate** in fun games, sports and activities with other kids

3. **Accept** and **Respect** other peoples' skin color, food, language, clothes, and ways of life

4. Be **Accountable** and **Reliable** to build trust and strong friendships

A friend is someone who thinks you're a good egg, even though you might be slightly cracked!

MAKING GOOD CENTS

Most children begin to receive money at an early age for all types of reasons, such as birthday presents, holiday gifts, allowances, good grades, and doing small jobs.

This Tooliez task will help you to think about how much things cost, choose what's most important, and plan how you'll be able to buy things you need and want.

Let's start by filling out the 3 items below. You can ask your parents or someone for help.

Item	Cost
1. My Needs:_____	$_____
2. My Wants:_____	$_____
3. My Dream Trip:_____	$_____

You must now make a big decision. Please choose <u>only</u> 1 of the 3 items you want to have the most:

Desired Item:_____ $_____

Great choice! Now it's time for you to figure out how you will pay for this item.

How much money do you have saved? $_____

How much more money do you need to buy your desired item? $_____

How can you earn extra money? (by doing chores, getting good grades, getting a job, etc.) _____

_____

How much money can you earn by doing these things? $_____

Now, how much do you still need to have the item of your choice? $_____

You're almost there! You've done some Tool-Rific planning. We hope you can ask your parents for suggestions on how to divide your money among savings, donations, investments and spending.

SPENDING WISELY
AS YOU SAVE SOME MONEY

You can spend your money on a variety of items.

Here are examples of reasons to SPEND money:

<u>Charity</u> – This is when you give your own money to help an organization.

<u>IOU</u> – This is an abbreviation for "I owe you." An I.O.U. is money that you borrow and must pay back.

<u>Spending Money</u> – This is money to buy fun items you want after your bills are paid.

Examples of reasons to SAVE money:

<u>Short–term Savings</u> – This is when you put money away for a short period of time to buy something that you want soon (and you don't have enough money right now).

<u>Long-term Savings</u> – This is when you save money for some years to pay for an expensive item.

Let's see how you can Spend and Save Five Dollars

Here's an example:

For Every Five Dollars Earned	$5.00
Long-Term Savings – College	– $0.50
Charity – Homeless Shelters	– $1.50
Short-Term Savings – Toys, Trips	– $0.50
Spending Money – Movies, Snacks	$2.50

And that's how you can SAVE and SPEND at the SAME TIME!!!

Let's face it, dividing up money you receive or earn may not always be easy to do. It will take a lot of discipline and self-control, so these are great tools to help plan for your future.

Now you're on your way to putting your own budget together!
The Tooliez hope this task makes a lot of cents to you!!!

KID FIT

Keep Your Body Clean, Healthy and Physically Strong.

Clean Daily

1. Take a bath or shower and clean all areas of your body
2. Wash your hands frequently, especially before you eat and after you use the bathroom
3. Brush, floss and rinse your teeth
4. Keep your finger and toe nails clean and trim
5. Wash your hair (as often as necessary)

Stay Healthy

1. Get fresh air
2. Go to bed early and get enough sleep to feel energized for the next day
3. Avoid smoking, drinking alcohol, and taking drugs
4. Avoid fighting, gangs, violent activities and any other negative behaviors

Eat from the Four Basic Food Groups

1. Dairy: Milk, cheese, ice cream and yogurt (2 to 3 servings a day)
2. Protein: Meats, fish, poultry and beans (2 to 3 servings a day)
3. Fruits and Vegetables: Apples, bananas, grapes, peaches, spinach, green beans (4 or more servings a day)
4. Wheats and Grains: Bread, cereals, rice and pasta (6 to 11 servings a day)

Get Plenty of Exercise

1. Push-ups strengthen your arms and chest
2. Sit-ups strengthen your stomach and back
3. Knee-bends strengthen your legs
4. Walking, jogging and running strengthen your heart, lungs and legs
5. Sporting activities build teamwork and strengthen your relationships with others

Safety

1. Never go outside or anywhere without your parents' permission and always stay within your parents' line of sight
2. When outside and away from your parents, make sure you have friends or family with you; never be alone
3. If you are ever separated from your parents or lost, stay calm and return to the original location where you were last with your parents
4. If a stranger grabs you, fall to the ground and scream for help as loudly as you can
5. If someone approaches you and says that your parents sent him to pick you up, always call your parents first to verify; never go anywhere or with anyone without your parents' knowledge or permission
6. Follow the rules
7. Use safety equipment

The TOOLIEZ™
Tool-Rific
SEVEN TOOLS FOR SUCCESS

Here are some helpful tips to motivate you to follow your desires.

1. **The DRILL** represents repetition. You must study or practice a skill over and over again in order to become very good at it. No pain, no gain!

2. **The HAMMER** stands for accuracy. You must focus on your task in order to perform and complete school work, chores and other tasks correctly. Ready, aim, strike your target!

3. **The SAW** signifies cutting out the negative and keeping the positive. You should cut out of your life anything that you do not need or does not make you a better person.

4. **The SCREWDRIVER** symbolizes standing your ground. You must take a stand for the values that you believe in, even when others have different beliefs or values. Hold firm and do not let others easily sway you!

5. **The RULER** stands for endurance. You must work hard and keep trying to achieve your goals. Don't give up on your dreams! You can go the distance.

6. **The WRENCH** represents connecting with others to help you achieve your goals. You can achieve much by yourself, but you can accomplish more when you team up with others. Embrace relationship-building and teamwork to go as far as you can imagine!

7. **The PAINTBRUSH** symbolizes renewal and rejuvenation. You may sometimes have to get rid of negative behaviors or influences in order to make room for fresh ideas and growth. Out with the old, in with the new!

The TOOLIEZ ™

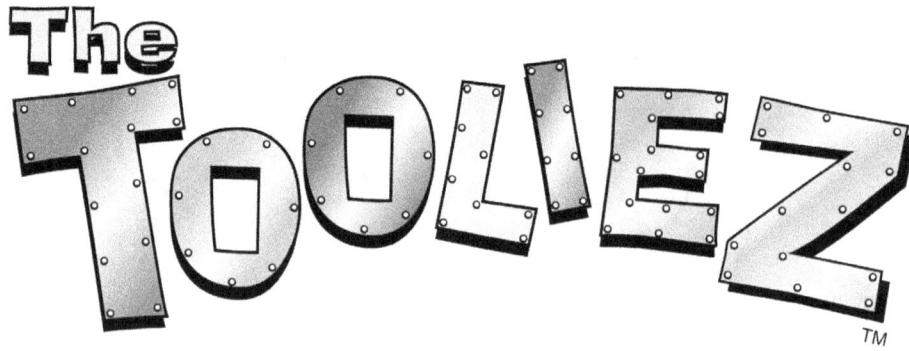

Tool-Rific Job List

A New Organizer for __All__ Ages!

*Develop good habits that will last a lifetime
and show your completed organizer to your parents!*

Name_____Date_____Age_____Grade_____

ONLY ✔ completed tasks

SPIRITUAL GROWTH	S	M	T	W	T	F	S
Study and practice my Faith							
Treat others the way I want to be treated							
Other:							
SELF CARE	S	M	T	W	T	F	S
Maintain a positive attitude							
Wash my hands (after I use the bathroom, after I play outside, before I eat)							
Brush my teeth (am/pm) and put away toothpaste							
Take a bath (hang towel and washcloth after bath)							
Keep hair clean, neat and groomed							
Dress myself (wear clean clothes, have a neat appearance)							
Place all worn clothes in laundry bin							
Lay out my school clothes							
Exercise and eat healthy meals and snacks							
Other:							

FAMILY	S	M	T	W	T	F	S
Obey my father and mother							
Teach and nurture my siblings							
Spend quality time with my family							
Communicate well (example: explain how I feel when I am mad)							
Clean up after meals and snacks							
Other:							
SCHOOL AND EXTRA-CURRICULAR ACTIVITIES	S	M	T	W	T	F	S
Follow rules and respect authority							
Complete homework and study hard							
Do not be afraid to ask for help when needed							
Play well with others (no bullying or fighting)							
Participate in sports and recreational activities							
Read books							
Take pride in today's lessons							
Remember to take lunch money, class notes, library books, paper and supplies to school							
Practice my special talents							
Perform community service							
Other:							
HOME	S	M	T	W	T	F	S
Complete my chores (clean my room, make my bed)							
Put away my clothes, shoes and toys							
Wash dishes and take out trash							
Clean the floors and carpet							
Clean bathroom							
Other:							

PARENTS AND CHILDREN: Please complete this section together.

Allowance Earned: $ _____

A Special Privilege I Would Like To Earn This Week:_____

_____

Sometimes your best reward is personal satisfaction in doing what is right.

Parent's Name:_____ Date:_____

Congratulations and Thank You

Congratulations and Thank you
For completing all your tasks
We knew that you could do it
We knew that you would pass.

Congratulations and Thank you
We're glad that you are done
We hope that you have learned something
We hope that you had fun.

Congratulations and Thank you
For trying something new
Now you are a Tool-Rific kid
We hope your dreams come true!

The TOOLIEZ ™

CERTIFICATE OF COMMITMENT

This is to recognize that:

_____

has completed The Tooliez Tool-Rific Character Building Activities for Kidz.

This certificate is awarded with the hope that you will continue to use the seven core character traits of The Tooliez and become a Tool-Rific person in your home, school and community.

CREATIVITY
HUMILITY
WISDOM
CONFIDENCE
RESPECT
HONESTY
DISCIPLINE

_____
Parent's Signature

_____
Reader's Signature

_____
Date

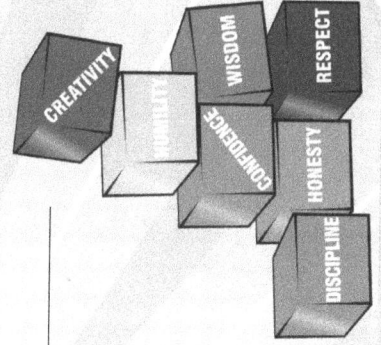

Tool-Rific Tools Create Tool-Rific Kidz

Tool-Rific CLUB